Freelance Freedom:

Mastering Remote Work and Building a Profitable Career

By

F.A. Ebenezer

Disclaimer

Copyright © by F. A. Ebenezer 2024. All rights reserved.

No part of this publication may be reproduced, stored in a retrieval system, or transmitted in any form or by any means, electronic, mechanical, photocopying, recording or otherwise, without the prior permission of the publisher.

Table of Contents:

Disclaimer 2
Table of Contents: 3
Introduction 8
    The Rise of Freelancing and Remote Work 8
    Why Freelancing is the Future of Work 9
    How to Use This Book 11
Chapter 1: Understanding the Freelance Landscape 14
    The Evolution of Freelancing 14
    Pros and Cons of Freelance Work 17
    Identifying Your Freelance Niche 19
Chapter 2: Setting Up for Success 23
    Creating a Professional Portfolio 23
    Crafting an Effective Resume and Cover Letter 25
    Building a Personal Brand 29
Chapter 3: Finding Your First Clients 34

Networking and Building Relationships 34
Leveraging Social Media for Client Acquisition
.... 37
Cold Pitching and Email Strategies 40
Chapter 4: Pricing Your Services 45
Understanding Market Rates 45
Creating Packages and Retainers 47
Negotiation Techniques 50
Chapter 5: Delivering Quality Work 55
Managing Client Expectations 55
Ensuring Consistent Quality 58
Gathering and Utilizing Feedback 61
Chapter 6: Major Freelance Platforms 65
Overview of Upwork, Fiverr, and Freelancer .. 65
Pros and Cons of Each Platform 69
Tips for Creating Winning Profiles 72
Chapter 7: Niche and Industry-Specific Platforms
.... 77

    Creative Platforms like 99designs and Behance 77

    Tech-Specific Platforms like Toptal and GitHub Jobs 81

    Writing and Content Platforms like ProBlogger and Contena 84

Chapter 8: Remote Job Boards 89

    General Remote Job Boards like Remote.co and We Work Remotely 89

    Industry-Specific Remote Job Boards 93

    How to Stand Out on Job Boards 95

Chapter 9: Leveraging Social Media and Networking Sites 100

    Using LinkedIn for Remote Opportunities 100

    Twitter, Facebook Groups, and Other Social Media 104

    Networking Best Practices 107

Chapter 10: Time Management and Productivity 110

Planning and Scheduling Your Workday 110

Tools for Time Tracking and Project Management 113

Avoiding Burnout 116

Chapter 11: Organizing Your Work 120

Managing Multiple Clients and Projects 120

Creating Efficient Workflows 122

Documenting Processes and Procedures 124

Tools for Organization and Efficiency 126

Chapter 12: Financial Management for Freelancers 130

Budgeting and Saving 130

Invoicing and Getting Paid on Time 133

Taxes and Legal Considerations 135

Chapter 13: Maintaining Work-Life Balance ... 139

Setting Boundaries and Expectations 139

Finding Time for Personal Growth and Learning 142

Balancing Work and Personal Life 145

Chapter 14: Scaling Your Freelance Business . 148
- Hiring Subcontractors and Virtual Assistants 148
- Expanding Your Service Offerings 151
- Long-Term Planning and Goal Setting 153
  - Conclusion 156

Chapter 15: Conclusion 158
- Reflecting on Your Freelance Journey 158
- Future Trends in Freelancing and Remote Work 160
- Resources for Continued Learning and Growth 163
  - Conclusion 166

Introduction

The Rise of Freelancing and Remote Work

In recent years, the landscape of work has undergone a dramatic transformation. Traditional office jobs, with their rigid schedules and fixed locations, are being replaced by more flexible and dynamic forms of employment. At the forefront of this revolution is freelancing and remote work. Fueled by advancements in technology and a global shift in work culture, more people than ever are opting to freelance or work remotely, enjoying the freedom and flexibility it offers.

The rise of the gig economy has contributed significantly to this shift. According to recent studies, over a third of the global workforce is now involved in some form of freelancing or gig work.

This trend is not limited to specific industries; it spans from creative fields like writing and design to technical sectors such as software development and digital marketing.

The internet has made it possible for freelancers to connect with clients worldwide, breaking down geographical barriers and opening up a plethora of opportunities.

Remote work, too, has seen a surge in popularity. The COVID-19 pandemic accelerated this trend, as companies were forced to adapt to remote operations. What started as a necessity has now become a preferred mode of work for many. Companies have realized the benefits of remote work, including reduced overhead costs, access to a broader talent pool, and increased employee satisfaction. As a result, remote work is here to stay, reshaping how businesses operate and how people approach their careers.

Why Freelancing is the Future of Work

Freelancing represents a fundamental shift in how we think about work. It offers a level of autonomy and flexibility that traditional employment often lacks. Freelancers have the freedom to choose their projects, set their schedules, and work from anywhere in the world. This level of control is particularly appealing to those seeking a better work-life balance, allowing them to tailor their work around their personal lives rather than the other way around.

Moreover, freelancing empowers individuals to capitalize on their unique skills and passions. Unlike traditional jobs that may require a wide range of responsibilities, freelancing allows you to specialize and become an expert in your chosen field. This specialization can lead to higher earning potential and greater job satisfaction, as freelancers are often more engaged and motivated when working on projects they are passionate about.

The future of work is also influenced by changing attitudes towards job security and career progression.

The traditional model of lifelong employment with a single company is becoming less common. Instead, people are seeking diverse experiences and multiple income streams. Freelancing aligns perfectly with this mindset, offering the opportunity to work on varied projects with different clients, continually learning and growing in the process.

Additionally, companies are increasingly recognizing the value of freelancers. Hiring freelancers allows businesses to access specialized skills on a project-by-project basis, providing flexibility and cost savings. This shift towards a more flexible workforce is transforming industries and creating new opportunities for freelancers worldwide.

How to Use This Book

"Freelance Freedom: Mastering Remote Work and Building a Profitable Career" is designed to be your comprehensive guide to navigating the world of freelancing and remote work.

Whether you're a seasoned freelancer looking to scale your business or a newcomer eager to break into the field, this book provides valuable insights and practical advice to help you succeed.

This book is divided into three main parts:

1. **Building a Profitable Freelance Career**: This section covers the foundational aspects of freelancing, from understanding the freelance landscape to setting up for success and finding your first clients. You'll learn how to price your services, deliver quality work, and build a sustainable career.
2. **Top Platforms for Finding Remote Work**: Here, we delve into the various platforms and job boards where you can find freelance and remote work opportunities. You'll discover the pros and cons of major platforms, tips for creating winning profiles, and strategies for leveraging social media and networking sites.
3. **Balancing Multiple Freelance Gigs and Projects**: Managing multiple clients and projects can be challenging.

This section provides practical tips on time management, productivity, financial management, and maintaining work-life balance. You'll also learn how to scale your freelance business and plan for long-term success.

Throughout the book, you'll find real-world examples, actionable tips, and resources to help you implement the strategies discussed. Each chapter is designed to build on the previous one, guiding you step-by-step through the process of becoming a successful freelancer and remote worker.

By the end of this book, you'll have the knowledge and tools to build a profitable freelance career, find the best remote work opportunities, and balance multiple projects effectively. Welcome to the future of work – your journey to freelance freedom starts here.

Chapter 1: Understanding the Freelance Landscape

The Evolution of Freelancing

Freelancing, once considered a fringe employment option, has evolved into a mainstream career choice embraced by millions worldwide. The concept of freelancing dates back centuries, with artisans and craftsmen working independently long before the advent of modern employment structures. However, the contemporary notion of freelancing as we know it began to take shape in the late 20th century, spurred by technological advancements and changing work dynamics.

In the 1990s, the rise of the internet revolutionized freelancing. Suddenly, individuals could connect with clients and employers beyond their localities, opening up a global marketplace for their skills.

Early platforms like Elance and oDesk (which later merged to form Upwork) provided the infrastructure for freelancers to find work, communicate with clients, and receive payments securely.

This period marked the beginning of the gig economy, where short-term contracts and freelance work started to gain traction.

The 21st century has seen an exponential growth in freelancing, driven by several key factors:

1. **Technological Advancements**: The proliferation of high-speed internet, cloud computing, and collaboration tools has made it easier than ever for freelancers to work remotely. Tools like Slack, Trello, and Zoom have bridged the communication gap, allowing seamless collaboration between freelancers and clients.
2. **Economic Shifts**: Economic uncertainties and the rise of startup culture have led businesses to seek more flexible workforce solutions.

Hiring freelancers allows companies to access specialized skills without the long-term commitment of full-time employment.

3. **Changing Work Preferences**: Millennials and Gen Z workers prioritize flexibility, work-life balance, and purpose-driven work. Freelancing offers these advantages, making it an attractive option for younger generations entering the workforce.
4. **Global Connectivity**: Freelancers can now work with clients from any part of the world. This globalization has expanded opportunities, allowing freelancers to tap into diverse markets and industries.

The evolution of freelancing continues as new technologies and work paradigms emerge. Today, freelancing encompasses a wide range of professions, from creative fields like writing and design to technical sectors such as software development and digital marketing.

Pros and Cons of Freelance Work

Like any career path, freelancing comes with its own set of advantages and challenges. Understanding these can help you make an informed decision about whether freelancing is the right fit for you.

Pros:

1. **Flexibility**: Freelancers have the freedom to set their own schedules and choose where they work. This flexibility is particularly beneficial for those seeking a better work-life balance or juggling personal commitments.
2. **Autonomy**: Freelancers have control over the projects they take on, the clients they work with, and the rates they charge. This autonomy allows for greater job satisfaction and the ability to align work with personal interests and values.
3. **Diverse Opportunities**: Freelancing offers exposure to a variety of projects and industries.

This diversity can lead to a more dynamic and fulfilling career, as freelancers continually learn and grow through new experiences.

4. **Potential for Higher Earnings**: Successful freelancers can often earn more than their traditionally employed counterparts, especially when they specialize in high-demand skills and build a strong client base.
5. **Location Independence**: Freelancers can work from anywhere, whether it's a home office, a co-working space, or a different country. This geographic freedom is a significant draw for many people.

Cons:

1. **Income Instability**: Unlike salaried employees, freelancers face fluctuating income levels. There may be periods of feast and famine, requiring careful financial planning and budgeting.
2. **Lack of Benefits**:

Freelancers do not receive traditional employment benefits such as health insurance, retirement plans, or paid leave. They must manage these aspects independently.
3. **Isolation**: Working alone can be isolating, especially for those who thrive in social environments. Freelancers need to make a conscious effort to stay connected with peers and professional networks.
4. **Client Management**: Freelancers are responsible for finding and retaining clients, managing contracts, and ensuring timely payments. This aspect of freelancing requires strong business and interpersonal skills.
5. **Work-Life Boundaries**: The flexibility of freelancing can blur the lines between work and personal life. Setting clear boundaries and maintaining a structured routine is essential to avoid burnout.

Identifying Your Freelance Niche

One of the keys to building a successful freelance career is identifying your niche. A niche is a specialized segment of the market where you can position yourself as an expert and attract clients who need your specific skills. Here's how to identify and refine your freelance niche:

1. **Assess Your Skills and Interests**: Start by listing your skills, experiences, and interests. Consider both your professional expertise and personal passions. The intersection of these areas can provide valuable insights into potential niches.
2. **Research Market Demand**: Analyze the market to identify in-demand skills and services. Use freelance platforms, job boards, and industry reports to understand what clients are looking for. High-demand niches often offer more opportunities and better rates.
3. **Evaluate the Competition**: Study other freelancers operating in your potential niche. Look at their profiles, services, and client feedback.

Identifying gaps in the market or areas where you can offer a unique value proposition will help you stand out.

4. **Define Your Unique Selling Proposition (USP)**: Your USP is what sets you apart from other freelancers. It could be a unique combination of skills, a specific approach to your work, or a particular style. Clearly articulating your USP will attract clients who resonate with your offering.
5. **Test and Refine**: Start offering your services in your chosen niche and gather feedback from clients. Use this feedback to refine your services, adjust your pricing, and hone your marketing strategy. Flexibility and adaptability are crucial in finding the perfect niche.
6. **Build a Portfolio**: Create a portfolio showcasing your work in your niche. Highlight successful projects, client testimonials, and any relevant credentials. A strong portfolio is essential for attracting new clients and establishing credibility.

Identifying and cultivating a niche allows you to position yourself as an expert, command higher rates, and attract clients who value your specialized skills. It's a strategic step towards building a profitable and sustainable freelance career.

By understanding the freelance landscape, weighing the pros and cons, and identifying your niche, you are laying a solid foundation for your freelance journey. In the following chapters, we will delve deeper into the practical aspects of building a successful freelance career, finding clients, and managing your work effectively.

Chapter 2: Setting Up for Success

Creating a Professional Portfolio

A professional portfolio is a critical tool for any freelancer. It showcases your skills, experience, and the quality of your work, helping potential clients understand what you bring to the table. Here's how to create a compelling portfolio that stands out:

1. Choose the Right Platform

Select a platform that best suits your industry and showcases your work effectively. For creatives, platforms like Behance, Dribbble, or a personal website work well. For writers, a Medium profile or a custom blog can be ideal. Developers might use GitHub to display their code.

2. Highlight Your Best Work

Quality over quantity is key.

Choose a selection of your best projects that demonstrate your range and expertise. Each piece should include a brief description of the project, your role, and the outcomes or impact of your work.

3. Include Case Studies

Case studies provide a detailed look at your process and the results you've achieved. They should outline the client's problem, your approach to solving it, and the success metrics or outcomes. Case studies help potential clients understand your problem-solving skills and the value you can bring to their projects.

4. Gather Testimonials

Client testimonials add credibility to your portfolio. Reach out to past clients and ask for feedback that you can include in your portfolio. Positive testimonials highlight your reliability, expertise, and the quality of your work.

5. Keep It Updated

Your portfolio should evolve as you complete new projects. Regularly update it with your latest work to reflect your current skills and capabilities. An up-to-date portfolio shows that you are active and engaged in your field.

6. Make It Easy to Navigate

A well-organized portfolio is essential. Group similar projects together and use clear headings and navigation. Potential clients should be able to quickly find the information they need without getting lost in a sea of content.

Crafting an Effective Resume and Cover Letter

While your portfolio showcases your work, your resume and cover letter provide a snapshot of your professional background and introduce you to potential clients. Here's how to craft each element effectively:

1. Writing Your Resume

a. Start with a Strong Summary

Begin with a brief summary that highlights your key skills, experience, and what makes you unique. This should be concise and compelling, drawing the reader in to learn more about you.

b. List Relevant Experience

Include your most relevant freelance and employment experiences. Focus on roles and projects that align with the services you offer. For each entry, provide a brief description of your responsibilities and achievements.

c. Highlight Skills and Certifications

Create a section for your key skills, both technical and soft skills. Include any relevant certifications, courses, or training that enhance your qualifications.

d. Showcase Accomplishments

Quantify your accomplishments wherever possible. Use metrics to demonstrate the impact of your work, such as "Increased website traffic by 50% through SEO optimization" or "Managed a project with a budget of $100,000."

e. Keep It Concise

A resume should be concise and to the point. Aim for one to two pages, focusing on the most important and relevant information. Use bullet points and clear headings to make it easy to read.

2. Crafting Your Cover Letter

a. Personalize Each Letter

Tailor your cover letter to the specific client and project. Mention the client's name and the project you're applying for. Personalization shows that you've done your research and are genuinely interested in the opportunity.

b. Start with a Strong Opening

Grab the reader's attention with a strong opening statement. Explain why you are interested in the project and what makes you the ideal candidate.

c. Highlight Relevant Experience

Briefly summarize your relevant experience and how it aligns with the client's needs. Use specific examples from your portfolio that demonstrate your skills and accomplishments.

d. Showcase Your Enthusiasm

Express your enthusiasm for the project and the client's business. Show that you understand their needs and are excited about the opportunity to contribute.

e. End with a Call to Action

Conclude your cover letter with a call to action. Invite the client to review your portfolio, discuss the project further, or schedule a meeting. Provide your contact information and express your eagerness to hear back.

Building a Personal Brand

Your personal brand is how you present yourself to the world. It encompasses your professional identity, the value you offer, and how you communicate with clients and the broader community. Here's how to build a strong personal brand:

1. Define Your Brand

a. Identify Your Unique Value Proposition

What sets you apart from other freelancers? Identify your unique strengths, skills, and the specific value you bring to clients. This could be your specialized expertise, your creative approach, or your outstanding customer service.

b. Know Your Target Audience

Understand who your ideal clients are and what they need. Tailor your branding to resonate with this audience, addressing their pain points and showcasing how you can solve their problems.

2. Create a Consistent Visual Identity

a. Design a Professional Logo

A professional logo is a key element of your brand's visual identity. It should be simple, memorable, and reflective of your brand's personality.

b. Choose Brand Colors and Fonts

Select a color palette and fonts that align with your brand's tone and message. Consistency in these elements across your website, social media, and marketing materials helps create a cohesive brand identity.

3. Establish an Online Presence

a. Build a Professional Website

Your website is your digital storefront. It should include your portfolio, resume, testimonials, and a blog or resources section if relevant.

Ensure it's user-friendly, visually appealing, and optimized for search engines.

b. Utilize Social Media

Choose social media platforms that are popular with your target audience and regularly share valuable content. This could include industry insights, project updates, or tips and advice. Engage with your audience by responding to comments and messages.

4. Communicate Your Brand Message

a. Develop a Tagline

Create a memorable tagline that encapsulates your brand's value proposition. It should be short, catchy, and easy to remember.

b. Share Your Story

Your personal story can humanize your brand and make it more relatable. Share your journey, your passion for your work, and what drives you.

Authenticity resonates with clients and helps build trust.

5. Network and Build Relationships

a. Attend Industry Events

Networking is crucial for building your brand. Attend industry events, conferences, and meetups to connect with potential clients and peers. Networking helps you stay updated on industry trends and expands your professional circle.

b. Join Online Communities

Participate in online communities related to your field. This could be forums, LinkedIn groups, or social media communities. Share your knowledge, ask questions, and build relationships with other professionals.

6. Continuously Improve and Evolve

a. Seek Feedback

Regularly seek feedback from clients and peers to understand how you can improve. Use this feedback to refine your services and enhance your brand.

b. Stay Updated

Stay updated with industry trends, new tools, and best practices. Continuously learning and adapting helps you stay relevant and competitive in the freelance market.

By creating a professional portfolio, crafting an effective resume and cover letter, and building a strong personal brand, you set yourself up for success in the freelancing world. These elements not only help you attract and retain clients but also establish your reputation and credibility in your field.

Chapter 3: Finding Your First Clients

Networking and Building Relationships

Building a successful freelance career often begins with effective networking and relationship-building. These connections can lead to your first clients and provide ongoing opportunities for collaboration and growth. Here's how to network effectively and build lasting professional relationships:

1. Attend Industry Events

a. Conferences and Trade Shows

Industry conferences and trade shows are excellent opportunities to meet potential clients and other professionals. Attend events relevant to your field, participate in sessions, and engage in conversations. Prepare an elevator pitch to succinctly explain who you are and what you do.

b. Local Meetups and Workshops

Local meetups and workshops provide a more intimate setting for networking. These events allow you to connect with professionals in your area, share experiences, and learn from others. They are also great for building a local client base.

2. Join Professional Organizations

Professional organizations offer numerous networking opportunities, from events and conferences to online forums and newsletters. Membership in these organizations can also enhance your credibility and provide access to valuable resources and industry insights.

3. Leverage Online Networking

a. LinkedIn

LinkedIn is a powerful tool for networking and client acquisition. Optimize your profile, join industry-specific groups, and actively participate in discussions.

Connect with potential clients, colleagues, and industry leaders. Share relevant content and engage with posts to increase your visibility.

b. Online Communities and Forums

Participate in online communities and forums related to your field. Platforms like Reddit, Quora, and specialized industry forums allow you to share your knowledge, answer questions, and connect with potential clients. Be active and provide valuable insights to build your reputation.

4. Nurture Existing Relationships

a. Follow Up and Stay in Touch

Keep in touch with people you meet at networking events and online. Follow up with a personalized message or email, and maintain regular contact. This helps keep you on their radar for future opportunities.

b. Provide Value

Offer help and share valuable information with your network without expecting immediate returns. This could include sharing industry insights, referring business, or providing feedback on a project. Building relationships based on mutual benefit and trust can lead to long-term professional connections.

Leveraging Social Media for Client Acquisition

Social media is a powerful tool for freelancers to showcase their work, connect with potential clients, and build their brand. Here's how to effectively use social media for client acquisition:

1. Choose the Right Platforms

Identify the social media platforms that are most popular with your target audience. For example, LinkedIn is ideal for B2B services, Instagram works well for visual creatives, and Twitter is great for tech and content professionals.

2. Optimize Your Profiles

Ensure that your social media profiles are professional and aligned with your brand. Use a clear and professional profile picture, write a compelling bio that highlights your skills and services, and include a link to your portfolio or website.

3. Share Valuable Content

a. Showcase Your Work

Regularly share examples of your work, including project highlights, case studies, and testimonials. Visual content tends to perform well, so include images, videos, and graphics where possible.

b. Share Industry Insights

Position yourself as an expert in your field by sharing industry insights, tips, and trends. This not only demonstrates your knowledge but also helps attract followers who are interested in your expertise.

4. Engage with Your Audience

a. Respond to Comments and Messages

Engage with your audience by responding to comments and messages promptly. This shows that you are approachable and interested in building relationships.

b. Participate in Discussions

Join conversations and discussions in your industry. Comment on relevant posts, share your opinions, and ask questions. This increases your visibility and helps establish your presence in the community.

5. Use Hashtags Strategically

Research and use relevant hashtags to increase the visibility of your posts. Hashtags help your content reach a wider audience and attract potential clients who are searching for specific services or topics.

7. Run Targeted Ads

Consider running targeted ads on platforms like Facebook, Instagram, and LinkedIn to reach potential clients. These ads can be tailored to specific demographics, industries, and interests, helping you attract the right audience.

Cold Pitching and Email Strategies

Cold pitching is a proactive approach to finding clients by reaching out directly to potential clients. While it can be challenging, a well-crafted pitch can open doors to new opportunities. Here's how to create effective cold pitches and email strategies:

1. Research Potential Clients

Before sending a pitch, research potential clients thoroughly. Understand their business, needs, and challenges. Identify how your services can provide value to them. Personalized pitches based on thorough research are more likely to be well-received.

2. Craft a Compelling Subject Line

The subject line is the first thing your potential client will see. Make it compelling and relevant to increase the chances of your email being opened. Keep it concise and to the point, and avoid generic phrases like "Freelance Services" or "Business Inquiry."

3. Write a Personalized Introduction

Begin your email with a personalized introduction that shows you've done your homework. Mention the recipient's name, their company, and a specific detail about their business or recent work. This demonstrates your genuine interest and sets you apart from generic pitches.

4. Clearly State Your Value Proposition

In the body of your email, clearly state what you can offer and how it will benefit the client. Focus on the value you bring and the specific problems you can solve. Use bullet points or short paragraphs to make your email easy to read.

6. Include Relevant Examples of Your Work

Include links to your portfolio or attach examples of your work that are relevant to the client's industry or needs. Demonstrating your expertise with tangible examples increases your credibility.

6. End with a Call to Action

Conclude your email with a clear call to action. This could be a request for a meeting, a phone call, or permission to send more information. Make it easy for the client to take the next step.

7. Follow Up

If you don't receive a response, follow up after a week or two. Keep your follow-up email short and polite, reiterating your interest and the value you can offer. Persistence shows your determination and professionalism.

Sample Cold Pitch Email

Subject: Helping [Client's Company] Enhance [Specific Need]

Hi [Client's Name],

I hope this email finds you well. My name is [Your Name], and I'm a freelance [Your Profession] with [X] years of experience in [Industry/Field]. I recently came across [Client's Company] and was impressed by your work on [Specific Project/Aspect].

I specialize in [Your Service] and have helped businesses like yours achieve [Specific Outcome]. For example, I recently worked with [Previous Client] to [Describe a Relevant Project or Result]. I believe my skills in [Specific Skill] could help [Client's Company] [Achieve a Specific Goal].

I've attached a few examples of my work and would love to discuss how I can support your upcoming projects. Are you available for a brief call next week to explore this further?

Thank you for your time, and I look forward to the possibility of working together.

Best regards, [Your Name] [Your Contact Information] [Link to Portfolio]

By effectively networking, leveraging social media, and using targeted cold pitching strategies, you can find your first clients and build a strong foundation for your freelance career. These methods will help you connect with potential clients, showcase your value, and secure projects that align with your skills and interests.

Chapter 4: Pricing Your Services

Understanding Market Rates

Setting the right price for your freelance services is crucial for attracting clients while ensuring you're fairly compensated for your work. Understanding market rates involves researching industry standards and adjusting based on your experience, skills, and niche.

1. Research Industry Standards

a. Use Online Resources

Websites like Glassdoor, Payscale, and industry-specific platforms often provide salary and rate information. These resources can give you a baseline understanding of what others in your field are charging.

b. Freelance Platforms

Platforms like Upwork, Fiverr, and Freelancer allow you to see what other freelancers in your niche are charging.

Examine profiles of top-rated freelancers to understand how they price their services.

c. Industry Reports

Look for industry reports and surveys that provide insights into average freelance rates. Organizations like the Freelancers Union often publish annual reports that detail current trends and average earnings.

2. Consider Your Experience and Skills

Your rates should reflect your level of experience and the unique skills you bring to the table. If you have specialized expertise, advanced degrees, or extensive experience, you can justify higher rates. Conversely, if you're just starting out, you might need to set lower rates initially and gradually increase them as you build your reputation and portfolio.

3. Adjust for Niche and Demand

Some niches command higher rates due to the specialized skills required or high demand. For instance, technical fields like software development or specialized areas like legal writing often have higher rates. Research your specific niche to understand where it falls on the pay scale.

4. Factor in Business Expenses

As a freelancer, you need to account for business expenses such as software, equipment, taxes, and health insurance. Ensure your rates cover these costs and allow you to earn a sustainable income.

Creating Packages and Retainers

Offering service packages and retainers can streamline your pricing and provide clients with clear options. Packages and retainers also help create predictable income streams for your freelance business.

1. Designing Service Packages

a. Bundle Your Services

Create packages that bundle your services at different levels. For example, if you're a web designer, you might offer a basic package with a simple website, a standard package with additional features, and a premium package with comprehensive services.

b. Define Deliverables Clearly

Each package should clearly outline the deliverables, timelines, and costs. Clients should easily understand what they're getting and how much it will cost. This transparency helps build trust and reduces the likelihood of scope creep.

c. Offer Value Additions

Include value additions in higher-tier packages to encourage clients to choose them. This could be additional revisions, faster delivery times, or extra features. Value additions should be appealing but manageable within your capacity.

2. Setting Up Retainers

a. Understand Retainer Agreements

Retainer agreements involve clients paying a set fee regularly (monthly, quarterly) for a predefined set of services. Retainers provide stability for freelancers and ensure ongoing support for clients.

b. Define Scope and Terms

Clearly define the scope of work covered by the retainer, including the number of hours or specific services. Outline the terms, such as payment schedule, contract length, and conditions for termination.

c. Offer Different Retainer Levels

Offer different retainer levels based on the client's needs. For example, a basic retainer might include a set number of hours per month, while a premium retainer offers more hours and additional services.

3. Benefits of Packages and Retainers

a. Predictable Income

Packages and retainers provide more predictable income compared to one-off projects. This financial stability allows you to plan and invest in your business more effectively.

b. Stronger Client Relationships

Ongoing engagements through retainers help build stronger relationships with clients. Long-term clients are more likely to refer you to others and provide consistent work.

c. Simplified Pricing

Packages and retainers simplify your pricing structure, making it easier for clients to understand and choose your services. This clarity can speed up the decision-making process and reduce negotiation time.

Negotiation Techniques

Effective negotiation is key to securing favorable rates and terms for your freelance services.

Here are some techniques to help you negotiate successfully:

1. Prepare Thoroughly

a. Know Your Worth

Be confident in the value you bring to the table. Understand your skills, experience, and the benefits you provide to clients. This confidence will help you stand firm during negotiations.

b. Research the Client

Understand the client's business, needs, and budget. Tailor your negotiation strategy to align with their priorities and demonstrate how your services can solve their specific problems.

2. Communicate Clearly

a. Start with Your Higher Rate

When discussing rates, start with the higher end of your pricing range.

This gives you room to negotiate and ensures you don't undervalue your services.

b. Articulate Your Value

Clearly communicate the value you offer. Highlight your unique skills, past successes, and how your work can positively impact the client's business. Use specific examples and metrics where possible.

3. Be Willing to Compromise

a. Offer Flexible Options

If the client's budget is a concern, offer flexible options such as adjusting the scope of work or suggesting alternative packages. This demonstrates your willingness to find a mutually beneficial solution.

b. Negotiate Non-Monetary Terms

Consider negotiating non-monetary terms, such as longer deadlines, reduced revisions, or future referrals. These concessions can make the deal more attractive without reducing your rate.

4. Set Boundaries

a. Know Your Limits

Know your bottom line and be prepared to walk away if the terms aren't favorable. Accepting a rate that's too low can lead to dissatisfaction and burnout.

b. Use a Contract

Always use a contract to formalize the agreement. Ensure it includes details on the scope of work, payment terms, deadlines, and any negotiated terms. A contract protects both you and the client and provides a clear reference if any disputes arise.

5. Follow Up and Build Relationships

a. Maintain Professionalism

Regardless of the negotiation outcome, maintain professionalism and courtesy. Building a positive relationship can lead to future opportunities or referrals.

b. Seek Feedback

If a negotiation doesn't go your way, seek feedback to understand the client's perspective. This information can help you refine your approach for future negotiations.

By understanding market rates, creating service packages and retainers, and mastering negotiation techniques, you can set competitive and fair prices for your freelance services. These strategies will help you attract clients, ensure you're adequately compensated, and build a sustainable freelance business.

Chapter 5: Delivering Quality Work

Managing Client Expectations

Managing client expectations is critical to delivering quality work and maintaining positive relationships. Clear communication and setting realistic expectations from the outset can prevent misunderstandings and ensure client satisfaction.

1. Clear Communication

a. Initial Consultation

Start with an initial consultation to understand the client's needs, goals, and expectations. Ask detailed questions to gather all necessary information and clarify any ambiguities. This helps you tailor your services to their specific requirements.

b. Detailed Proposals

Provide a detailed proposal outlining the scope of work, deliverables, timelines, and costs. Include any assumptions, dependencies, and limitations to ensure the client understands the project's boundaries.

c. Regular Updates

Keep clients informed throughout the project with regular updates. This could be through weekly progress reports, email updates, or scheduled meetings. Regular communication helps manage expectations and addresses any concerns promptly.

2. Setting Realistic Timelines

a. Assess Workload

Before committing to a timeline, assess your current workload and the complexity of the project. Provide a realistic timeframe that includes buffer time for revisions and unforeseen delays.

b. Underpromise and Overdeliver

It's better to underpromise and overdeliver than to miss deadlines. Set conservative deadlines that you're confident you can meet, and aim to deliver the work early if possible.

3. Defining Scope and Boundaries

a. Scope of Work

Clearly define the scope of work in your contract or proposal. Specify what is included and excluded, and outline any potential additional costs for out-of-scope work.

b. Change Management

Establish a process for handling changes or additional requests. Communicate the impact on timelines and costs upfront, and get written approval before proceeding with any changes.

4. Setting Payment Terms

a. Payment Milestones

Break down the payment into milestones tied to deliverables. This ensures you get paid for the work completed and provides the client with a clear understanding of when payments are due.

b. Upfront Deposits

Consider requiring an upfront deposit before starting work. This secures your commitment and covers initial costs.

Ensuring Consistent Quality

Consistent quality is key to building a reputation for reliability and excellence. Implementing processes and standards helps ensure that every project meets your high standards.

1. Develop Standard Operating Procedures (SOPs)

a. Document Processes

Document your processes for different types of projects.

SOPs ensure consistency and efficiency, and they serve as a reference for maintaining quality.

b. Use Checklists

Create checklists for each stage of the project to ensure no critical steps are missed. Checklists help maintain consistency and quality across all projects.

2. Implement Quality Control Measures

a. Peer Reviews

If possible, have another professional review your work before delivering it to the client. Fresh eyes can catch errors or suggest improvements you might have missed.

b. Client Reviews

Incorporate client reviews at key milestones. This allows clients to provide feedback and request adjustments early, ensuring the final deliverable meets their expectations.

3. Use Reliable Tools and Software

a. Project Management Tools

Use project management tools like Trello, Asana, or Monday.com to organize tasks, track progress, and collaborate with clients. These tools help streamline workflows and ensure nothing falls through the cracks.

b. Quality Assurance Tools

Utilize quality assurance tools relevant to your field. For example, Grammarly for writing, design proofing tools for visual projects, or code validation tools for development work.

4. Continual Learning and Improvement

a. Stay Updated

Keep your skills and knowledge up-to-date with the latest trends, tools, and best practices in your field. Continuous learning helps you deliver cutting-edge solutions to clients.

b. Reflect and Improve

After completing each project, reflect on what went well and what could be improved. Use this reflection to refine your processes and enhance the quality of your work.

Gathering and Utilizing Feedback

Feedback is invaluable for improving your services and building stronger client relationships. Actively seeking and utilizing feedback demonstrates your commitment to excellence and continuous improvement.

1. Soliciting Feedback

a. End-of-Project Surveys

Send a survey or questionnaire at the end of each project to gather client feedback. Ask specific questions about their satisfaction with the deliverables, communication, and overall experience.

b. Informal Check-ins

Throughout the project, check in informally with clients to gauge their satisfaction and address any concerns. This proactive approach can prevent small issues from becoming major problems.

2. Analyzing Feedback

a. Identify Patterns

Look for patterns in feedback across different projects. Common themes can indicate areas for improvement or highlight your strengths.

b. Categorize Feedback

Categorize feedback into actionable insights. Separate constructive criticism from positive feedback and prioritize areas that need improvement.

3. Implementing Changes

a. Action Plans

Develop action plans based on feedback. If clients consistently mention slow response times, for example, implement changes to improve your communication processes.

b. Communicate Improvements

Inform clients about the changes you've made based on their feedback. This shows that you value their input and are committed to improving your services.

4. Building a Feedback Loop

a. Continuous Improvement

Establish a continuous feedback loop by regularly seeking feedback from clients and making ongoing improvements. This iterative process helps you maintain high standards and adapt to changing client needs.

b. Client Testimonials and Case Studies

Positive feedback can be turned into testimonials and case studies for your portfolio. These endorsements build credibility and help attract new clients.

By effectively managing client expectations, ensuring consistent quality, and gathering and utilizing feedback, you can deliver outstanding work that meets and exceeds client expectations. These practices not only enhance your reputation but also lead to long-term client relationships and ongoing success in your freelance career.

Chapter 6: Major Freelance Platforms

Overview of Upwork, Fiverr, and Freelancer

Finding remote work has never been easier thanks to the myriad of online platforms connecting freelancers with clients. Three of the most popular platforms are Upwork, Fiverr, and Freelancer. Each platform has its unique features, advantages, and challenges.

1. Upwork

Upwork is one of the largest freelance marketplaces, offering a broad range of job categories, from web development and writing to marketing and customer service.

a. Features

- **Wide Range of Categories:**

Upwork supports a diverse array of job categories, making it suitable for almost any freelance profession.

- **Payment Protection:** Upwork offers payment protection for hourly and fixed-price contracts, ensuring freelancers get paid for their work.
- **Work Diary:** For hourly projects, freelancers can use Upwork's Work Diary to track time and provide clients with transparency.

b. How It Works

Freelancers create profiles showcasing their skills and experience. Clients post job listings, and freelancers can submit proposals for jobs they are interested in. Upwork also features a "Talent Marketplace" where clients can invite freelancers to apply for their jobs.

3. Fiverr

Fiverr is a platform where freelancers offer services (called "gigs") starting at $5. It's popular for quick, task-based projects.

a. Features

- **Service-Based Structure:** Freelancers create gigs detailing the services they offer, which clients can purchase directly.
- **Upselling Options:** Freelancers can offer additional services or upgrades for extra fees, allowing for higher earnings.
- **Buyer Requests:** Freelancers can respond to specific job requests posted by clients, increasing their chances of landing projects.

b. How It Works

Freelancers set up gigs describing their services, starting prices, and delivery times. Clients browse these gigs and place orders directly. Fiverr handles the transaction, and freelancers deliver the completed work through the platform.

4. Freelancer

Freelancer is a global marketplace that connects clients with freelancers for various types of projects.

a. Features

- **Contests:** In addition to traditional job postings, clients can run contests where freelancers submit work, and the winner gets paid.
- **Milestone Payments:** Similar to Upwork, Freelancer offers milestone payments to ensure freelancers get paid as they complete project phases.
- **Project Management Tools:** The platform provides tools for managing projects, communication, and payments.

b. How It Works

Freelancers create profiles and bid on projects posted by clients. Clients review bids and select the freelancer they want to hire.

Freelancer also allows freelancers to enter contests to win projects based on their submissions.

Pros and Cons of Each Platform

1. Upwork

Pros:

- **Large Client Base:** A vast number of clients post jobs regularly, increasing opportunities for freelancers.
- **Variety of Projects:** Offers a wide range of project types and categories.
- **Secure Payments:** Payment protection and dispute resolution services ensure reliable transactions.

Cons:

- **High Competition:** The large number of freelancers can make it challenging to stand out.
- **Service Fees:**

Upwork charges a service fee ranging from 5% to 20%, depending on your total billings with a client.

- **Proposal Limits:** Freelancers have a limited number of "connects" (tokens used to submit proposals), which can be restrictive.

2. Fiverr

Pros:

- **Easy to Start:** Simple setup process and immediate ability to create gigs.
- **Direct Sales:** Clients can purchase services directly, reducing the need for extensive bidding.
- **Flexibility:** Freelancers can offer a wide range of services and set their own prices.

Cons:

- **Low Starting Prices:** Many clients expect services at very low prices, which can undervalue your work.

- **High Competition:** Similar to Upwork, the large number of freelancers can make it difficult to attract clients.
- **Service Fees:** Fiverr charges a 20% service fee on all transactions, which can cut into your earnings.

3. Freelancer

Pros:

- **Diverse Opportunities:** Offers various project types, including one-off tasks and long-term contracts.
- **Global Reach:** Connects freelancers with clients from around the world, expanding potential job markets.
- **Contests:** Unique contest feature allows freelancers to showcase their skills and win projects.

Cons:

- **Service Fees:**

Freelancer charges fees for both bidding on projects and transaction commissions, which can add up.

- **Complex Interface:** The platform's interface can be overwhelming for new users.
- **High Competition:** Like the other platforms, high competition can make it challenging to secure jobs.

Tips for Creating Winning Profiles

1. Craft a Compelling Profile

a. Professional Photo

Use a high-quality, professional photo. A friendly, approachable image helps build trust with potential clients.

b. Clear and Concise Bio

Write a clear and concise bio that highlights your skills, experience, and what makes you unique. Focus on the value you bring to clients.

c. Showcase Your Work

Include a portfolio showcasing your best work. Use relevant examples that demonstrate your expertise and versatility.

2. Highlight Skills and Experience

a. Relevant Skills

List all relevant skills that align with the services you offer. This makes it easier for clients to find you when they search for specific skills.

b. Detailed Work History

Provide a detailed work history, including previous projects and client feedback. Highlight successful projects and key achievements.

3. Optimize for Search

a. Use Keywords

Incorporate relevant keywords throughout your profile.

This improves your visibility in search results when clients look for freelancers with your skills.

b. Update Regularly

Keep your profile updated with new skills, experiences, and portfolio pieces. Regular updates signal to the platform's algorithm that you are an active freelancer.

4. Gather Client Reviews

a. Request Feedback

After completing a project, ask clients for feedback and reviews. Positive reviews boost your credibility and attract more clients.

b. Display Testimonials

Feature testimonials prominently on your profile. Highlight reviews that speak to your professionalism, skills, and reliability.

5. Set Competitive Rates

a. Research Competitors

Research what other freelancers with similar skills and experience are charging. Set your rates competitively to attract clients while ensuring fair compensation.

b. Offer Introductory Rates

Consider offering introductory rates to build your client base and gather reviews. Once established, you can gradually increase your rates.

6. Maintain Professionalism

a. Prompt Communication

Respond to client inquiries and messages promptly. Timely communication demonstrates your professionalism and commitment.

b. Deliver Quality Work

Consistently deliver high-quality work on time.

Meeting or exceeding client expectations leads to positive reviews and repeat business.

By leveraging the strengths of major freelance platforms like Upwork, Fiverr, and Freelancer, and creating a compelling and optimized profile, you can increase your chances of finding remote work and building a successful freelance career. Understanding the pros and cons of each platform and utilizing effective strategies will help you stand out in a competitive market and attract valuable clients.

Chapter 7: Niche and Industry-Specific Platforms

In addition to the major freelance marketplaces, niche and industry-specific platforms can be valuable resources for finding remote work. These platforms cater to particular fields, offering opportunities tailored to specific skills and industries. By leveraging these specialized platforms, freelancers can find clients who value their expertise and are willing to pay a premium for specialized skills.

Creative Platforms like 99designs and Behance

Creative professionals, such as designers, illustrators, and photographers, can benefit from platforms that focus on visual and creative work.

1. 99designs

99designs is a platform specifically for designers, offering a unique way to connect with clients through design contests and direct hiring.

a. Features

- **Design Contests:** Clients create design briefs, and multiple designers submit their concepts. The client selects the winning design and awards the designer with a predetermined prize.
- **Direct Hiring:** Clients can also hire designers directly for one-on-one projects.
- **Portfolio Display:** Designers can showcase their portfolios to attract potential clients.

b. Pros

- **Exposure to Multiple Clients:** Design contests provide exposure to various clients simultaneously, increasing the chances of winning projects.
- **Creative Freedom:** Designers have the freedom to interpret briefs creatively and showcase their unique style.

- **High Earning Potential:** Winning multiple contests can lead to significant earnings and a strong reputation.

c. Cons

- **High Competition:** The contest model means designers often compete against many others, making it challenging to win consistently.
- **Spec Work:** Designers may spend time creating concepts without guaranteed payment unless they win.

2. Behance

Behance is a platform where creative professionals can showcase their portfolios, discover inspiration, and connect with potential clients.

a. Features

- **Portfolio Showcase:** Behance allows creatives to display their work in visually appealing portfolios.

- **Job Listings:** The platform features job listings and freelance opportunities from top companies and agencies.
- **Networking:** Creatives can follow and connect with other professionals, fostering a community of inspiration and collaboration.

b. Pros

- **Visibility:** A strong Behance profile can attract clients and job offers from around the world.
- **Creative Community:** The platform's community aspect allows for networking, collaboration, and feedback from peers.
- **Inspiration:** Access to a vast array of creative projects can inspire and motivate.

c. Cons

- **Passive Job Search:** While showcasing work can attract clients, it may not be as proactive as bidding on jobs or responding to direct listings.

- **Need for Strong Portfolio:** Success on Behance heavily relies on having a visually compelling and impressive portfolio.

Tech-Specific Platforms like Toptal and GitHub Jobs

For tech professionals, platforms focused on programming, development, and IT offer targeted opportunities to find remote work.

1. Toptal

Toptal is a highly selective platform that connects top freelancers with clients needing expert tech talent.

a. Features

- **Rigorous Screening:** Toptal's screening process ensures only the top 3% of applicants are accepted, guaranteeing high-quality freelancers.
- **High-Profile Clients:**

The platform works with notable clients, including Fortune 500 companies and startups.

- **Project Matching:** Toptal matches freelancers with projects that fit their skills and expertise.

b. Pros

- **High Earning Potential:** The platform's exclusivity allows freelancers to command premium rates.
- **Quality Projects:** Toptal offers access to high-quality, challenging projects from reputable clients.
- **Supportive Community:** Freelancers benefit from Toptal's network and resources, including community events and professional development opportunities.

c. Cons

- **Selective Entry:** The rigorous screening process can be a barrier for many freelancers.

- **High Expectations:** Toptal clients expect top-tier performance, which can be demanding.

2. GitHub Jobs

GitHub Jobs is a job board associated with GitHub, a platform widely used by developers for version control and collaboration.

a. Features

- **Targeted Job Listings:** GitHub Jobs focuses on developer roles, including remote opportunities.
- **Reputable Employers:** Many listings come from reputable tech companies and startups looking for skilled developers.
- **Integration with GitHub:** Freelancers can showcase their GitHub profiles and repositories to demonstrate their skills and experience.

b. Pros

- **Relevant Listings:** The job board caters specifically to developers, ensuring relevant and targeted opportunities.
- **Professional Credibility:** A strong GitHub profile can enhance a freelancer's credibility and attract potential clients.
- **Networking:** GitHub's community and collaborative features enable networking and skill development.

c. Cons

- **Limited Scope:** The job board is primarily focused on development roles, limiting opportunities for other tech specialties.
- **Competition:** Popularity among developers means high competition for listed jobs.

Writing and Content Platforms like ProBlogger and Contena

Writers and content creators can find numerous opportunities on platforms dedicated to writing and content creation.

1. ProBlogger

ProBlogger is a job board specifically for blogging and content writing roles, featuring listings from various industries.

a. Features

- **Targeted Job Listings:** The platform lists freelance, part-time, and full-time writing jobs.
- **Industry Variety:** Listings cover a wide range of topics, from tech and finance to lifestyle and travel.
- **Community Resources:** ProBlogger offers resources and tips for improving writing skills and building a successful freelance career.

b. Pros

- **Focused Listings:** The job board's focus on writing roles ensures relevant opportunities for content creators.

- **Industry Reach:** ProBlogger is well-known in the blogging community, attracting quality job listings.
- **Supportive Community:** Access to resources and a community of fellow writers.

c. Cons

- **Job Volume:** The number of listings can vary, leading to periods of fewer opportunities.
- **Competition:** High competition for desirable writing jobs.

2. Contena

Contena is a subscription-based platform that curates high-quality writing and content creation job listings.

a. Features

- **Curated Listings:** Contena provides a curated list of writing jobs, ensuring high-quality opportunities.

- **Job Alerts:** Subscribers receive job alerts tailored to their preferences and skills.
- **Training Resources:** The platform offers training resources and courses to help writers improve their skills and succeed in their freelance careers.

b. Pros

- **Quality Opportunities:** The curation process ensures access to high-quality and well-paying jobs.
- **Personalized Alerts:** Job alerts save time and help writers find opportunities that match their skills.
- **Professional Development:** Access to training and resources for career growth.

c. Cons

- **Subscription Cost:** The platform requires a subscription fee, which can be a barrier for some freelancers.
- **Limited Free Access:** Limited features are available without a subscription.

By utilizing niche and industry-specific platforms like 99designs, Behance, Toptal, GitHub Jobs, ProBlogger, and Contena, freelancers can find opportunities tailored to their skills and expertise. These platforms offer targeted job listings, valuable community resources, and the potential for high-quality projects and clients. Leveraging these specialized platforms can enhance a freelancer's career and open doors to new and exciting opportunities in their field.

Chapter 8: Remote Job Boards

In the digital age, remote job boards have become invaluable resources for finding remote work opportunities. These platforms cater to a wide range of industries and job roles, making it easier for freelancers and remote workers to connect with potential employers. In this chapter, we'll explore some of the most popular general and industry-specific remote job boards, and provide tips on how to stand out on these platforms.

General Remote Job Boards like Remote.co and We Work Remotely

General remote job boards cover a broad spectrum of job categories and industries, providing diverse opportunities for remote work.

1. Remote.co

Remote.co is a comprehensive remote job board that offers listings across various industries, including marketing, development, design, customer service, and more.

a. Features

- **Wide Range of Categories:** Remote.co covers a broad array of job categories, making it suitable for various professions.
- **Company Profiles:** The platform features profiles of companies that offer remote work, helping job seekers understand potential employers.
- **Remote Work Resources:** Remote.co provides resources, articles, and tips for remote workers.

b. Pros

- **Diverse Opportunities:** The platform's wide range of job categories provides numerous opportunities for remote work.
- **Company Insights:**

Company profiles offer valuable insights into potential employers.

- **Resourceful:** The additional resources and tips are beneficial for remote job seekers.

c. Cons

- **High Competition:** The popularity of the platform means high competition for listed jobs.
- **Less Frequent Updates:** Job listings may not be updated as frequently as some other platforms.

2. We Work Remotely

We Work Remotely is one of the largest remote job boards, connecting remote workers with employers across various fields.

a. Features

- **Large Job Pool:** The platform lists a vast number of remote jobs in multiple categories, including tech, design, sales, and more.

- **Global Reach:** Jobs are posted by companies from around the world, offering a global job market.
- **Community and Resources:** We Work Remotely offers a community forum and resources for remote workers.

b. Pros

- **Extensive Listings:** The large number of job listings increases the chances of finding suitable opportunities.
- **Global Opportunities:** The platform's global reach allows job seekers to find remote work regardless of their location.
- **Supportive Community:** The community forum and resources provide support and valuable information for remote workers.

c. Cons

- **High Competition:** The platform's popularity results in high competition for jobs.

- **Listing Quality:** The quality of job listings can vary, with some lower-quality or outdated posts.

Industry-Specific Remote Job Boards

In addition to general remote job boards, industry-specific platforms can offer more targeted opportunities for remote work.

1. Tech-Specific Remote Job Boards

- **Stack Overflow Jobs:** Focused on developer and tech roles, Stack Overflow Jobs connects tech professionals with remote opportunities.
- **AngelList:** Known for startup jobs, AngelList offers remote opportunities in tech and startup environments.

2. Writing and Content Remote Job Boards

- **BloggingPro:** A job board specifically for blogging and content writing roles, offering remote opportunities in various niches.
- **Freelance Writing Jobs:**

A platform dedicated to writing jobs, including remote freelance positions across different genres and industries.

3. Marketing and Sales Remote Job Boards

- **FlexJobs:** Although not industry-specific, FlexJobs offers a significant number of remote marketing and sales positions.
- **RemoteMarketingJobs.com:** Specializes in remote marketing jobs, providing targeted listings for marketing professionals.

4. Design and Creative Remote Job Boards

- **Dribbble:** Primarily a community for designers, Dribbble also features remote job listings for design roles.
- **DesignCrowd:** A platform for designers to find remote work opportunities through project listings and contests.

How to Stand Out on Job Boards

To succeed on remote job boards, it's essential to create a compelling presence that attracts potential employers. Here are some tips on how to stand out:

1. Optimize Your Profile

a. Professional Summary

Write a professional summary that highlights your skills, experience, and what makes you unique. Focus on your achievements and the value you bring to potential employers.

b. Detailed Experience

Provide detailed descriptions of your past work experience, including specific projects, roles, and responsibilities. Use quantifiable results to demonstrate your impact.

c. Skills and Certifications

List relevant skills and certifications that align with the job roles you're targeting. Highlight any specialized training or expertise.

2. Tailor Your Applications

a. Customized Cover Letters

Write customized cover letters for each job application. Address the specific requirements of the job and explain how your skills and experience make you the ideal candidate.

b. Relevant Resumes

Tailor your resume to match the job description. Emphasize relevant experience and skills that align with the job requirements.

3. Showcase Your Work

a. Portfolio

Create an online portfolio that showcases your best work.

Include case studies, project descriptions, and visual examples of your achievements.

b. Samples

If applicable, provide samples of your work directly in your job applications. This could include writing samples, design projects, or code repositories.

4. Leverage Keywords

a. Job Descriptions

Incorporate keywords from the job descriptions into your profile, resume, and cover letter. This helps your application get noticed by applicant tracking systems (ATS) and hiring managers.

b. Industry Terms

Use industry-specific terms and jargon that demonstrate your familiarity with the field. This shows that you understand the industry and its requirements.

5. Network and Engage

a. Online Communities

Join online communities and forums related to your industry. Engage in discussions, share your expertise, and connect with potential employers and peers.

b. Social Media

Leverage social media platforms like LinkedIn to network with professionals in your field. Share your work, participate in discussions, and build relationships with potential employers.

6. Continuous Improvement

a. Skill Development

Continuously update and expand your skill set. Take online courses, attend webinars, and stay current with industry trends and technologies.

b. Feedback and Adaptation

Seek feedback on your applications and profiles. Use constructive criticism to improve and adapt your approach to better meet the expectations of potential employers.

By leveraging general and industry-specific remote job boards, optimizing your profile, and employing effective application strategies, you can increase your chances of securing remote work opportunities. Standing out on these platforms requires a combination of showcasing your expertise, tailoring your applications, and actively engaging with the remote work community.

Chapter 9: Leveraging Social Media and Networking Sites

Social media and networking sites are powerful tools for finding remote work opportunities. By strategically using these platforms, you can connect with potential clients, showcase your skills, and stay updated on industry trends. In this chapter, we'll explore how to effectively leverage LinkedIn, Twitter, Facebook Groups, and other social media platforms for remote work, as well as best practices for networking.

Using LinkedIn for Remote Opportunities

LinkedIn is a professional networking site that serves as an essential resource for remote job seekers. With its vast network of professionals and companies, LinkedIn can help you find remote work opportunities, connect with potential clients, and build your professional brand.

1. Optimize Your LinkedIn Profile

a. Professional Photo and Headline

- **Professional Photo:** Use a high-quality, professional photo that conveys friendliness and competence.
- **Headline:** Craft a compelling headline that clearly states your profession and what you offer, such as "Remote Web Developer Specializing in E-commerce Solutions."

b. Detailed Summary

Write a detailed summary that highlights your skills, experience, and what makes you unique. Focus on your achievements and the value you bring to potential employers. Include keywords relevant to your industry to improve searchability.

c. Experience and Skills

- **Experience:** List your work experience with detailed descriptions of your roles, responsibilities, and achievements.

Use quantifiable results to demonstrate your impact.

- **Skills:** Add relevant skills to your profile. Endorse and get endorsements from colleagues to validate your expertise.

2. Build and Engage with Your Network

a. Connect with Relevant Professionals

Connect with professionals in your industry, including former colleagues, clients, and potential employers. Personalize connection requests to explain why you want to connect.

b. Join LinkedIn Groups

Join LinkedIn groups related to your field or remote work. Participate in discussions, share your insights, and connect with group members.

c. Engage with Content

- **Post Updates:** Regularly share updates about your projects, achievements, and industry insights.
- **Comment and Share:** Engage with posts from your connections by commenting and sharing valuable content. This increases your visibility and demonstrates your expertise.

3. Utilize LinkedIn Job Search Features

a. Job Alerts

Set up job alerts for remote opportunities that match your skills and preferences. LinkedIn will notify you of relevant job postings.

b. Apply for Jobs

Apply for remote jobs directly through LinkedIn. Tailor your applications to match the job descriptions and highlight your relevant experience.

c. LinkedIn ProFinder

Consider joining LinkedIn ProFinder, a platform that connects freelancers with clients seeking specific services. Create a ProFinder profile and respond to project proposals to find remote work opportunities.

Twitter, Facebook Groups, and Other Social Media

In addition to LinkedIn, other social media platforms like Twitter and Facebook Groups can also be valuable resources for finding remote work and networking.

1. Twitter

a. Build Your Profile

- **Professional Bio:** Write a concise bio that highlights your skills and what you offer. Include relevant hashtags to increase your visibility.
- **Profile Photo and Banner:** Use a professional photo and a banner that reflects your personal brand.

b. Follow Relevant Accounts

Follow industry leaders, companies, and hashtags related to remote work and your field. This will keep you updated on job opportunities and industry trends.

c. Engage with Content

- **Tweet Regularly:** Share insights, updates, and relevant content to demonstrate your expertise.
- **Retweet and Comment:** Engage with tweets from industry leaders and potential clients by retweeting and commenting thoughtfully.

d. Use Hashtags

Use hashtags like #RemoteWork, #Freelance, and #JobSearch to discover remote job opportunities and make your tweets more discoverable.

2. Facebook Groups

a. Join Relevant Groups

Join Facebook groups dedicated to remote work, freelancing, and your specific industry. These groups often share job postings and valuable resources.

b. Participate Actively

- **Engage in Discussions:** Contribute to discussions by sharing your insights and answering questions.
- **Post About Your Services:** Occasionally post about your services and expertise to let group members know what you offer.

c. Network with Members

Connect with group members by sending friend requests and engaging with their content. Building relationships can lead to job opportunities and referrals.

3. Other Social Media Platforms

a. Instagram

Use Instagram to showcase your work visually. Share portfolio pieces, behind-the-scenes content, and success stories to attract potential clients.

b. YouTube

Create a YouTube channel to share tutorials, industry insights, and case studies. This positions you as an expert in your field and can attract clients who value your knowledge.

Networking Best Practices

Networking is crucial for finding remote work and building a successful freelance career. Here are some best practices to help you network effectively:

1. Be Genuine and Authentic

Approach networking with a genuine interest in building relationships rather than just seeking opportunities. Authentic interactions build trust and long-term connections.

2. Offer Value

Provide value to your connections by sharing useful information, offering assistance, and supporting their projects. This establishes you as a valuable contact and increases the likelihood of reciprocity.

3. Follow Up

After meeting someone new, follow up with a personalized message to reinforce the connection. Express your appreciation for the interaction and suggest ways to stay in touch.

4. Attend Virtual Events

Participate in webinars, online conferences, and virtual networking events related to your industry. These events provide opportunities to meet new contacts and learn from industry experts.

5. Leverage Mutual Connections

Ask mutual connections for introductions to potential clients or collaborators. A warm introduction from a trusted contact can significantly enhance your credibility.

6. Maintain an Active Online Presence

Regularly update your social media profiles, share content, and engage with your network. Consistent activity keeps you on the radar of potential clients and collaborators.

By leveraging social media and networking sites like LinkedIn, Twitter, and Facebook Groups, and following best practices for networking, you can expand your professional network, attract remote work opportunities, and build a successful freelance career. Effective use of these platforms requires a strategic approach, consistent engagement, and a focus on building genuine relationships.

Chapter 10: Time Management and Productivity

Balancing multiple freelance gigs and projects requires excellent time management and productivity skills. By planning and scheduling your workday effectively, using the right tools, and taking steps to avoid burnout, you can maintain a high level of performance and deliver quality work to all your clients.

Planning and Scheduling Your Workday

1. Set Clear Goals

Start by setting clear, achievable goals for each project. Break down larger goals into smaller, manageable tasks. This helps you stay focused and motivated.

2. Prioritize Tasks

a. Eisenhower Matrix

Use the Eisenhower Matrix to prioritize tasks based on urgency and importance:

- **Urgent and Important:** Do these tasks immediately.
- **Important but Not Urgent:** Schedule these tasks for later.
- **Urgent but Not Important:** Delegate these tasks if possible.
- **Not Urgent and Not Important:** Eliminate these tasks to free up time.

b. ABCDE Method

Use the ABCDE method to categorize tasks:

- **A:** Must-do tasks with serious consequences if not completed.
- **B:** Should-do tasks with mild consequences if not completed.
- **C:** Nice-to-do tasks with no real consequences if not completed.
- **D:** Delegate tasks.
- **E:** Eliminate tasks that are not necessary.

3. Create a Daily Schedule

a. Time Blocking

Time blocking involves dividing your day into blocks of time, each dedicated to a specific task or project. This method helps you stay focused and reduces the time spent switching between tasks.

b. Buffer Time

Include buffer time between tasks to accommodate unexpected delays and to allow for breaks. This prevents your schedule from becoming too rigid and helps you stay on track.

4. Set Boundaries

a. Work Hours

Set clear work hours and stick to them. This helps you maintain a work-life balance and ensures that you have dedicated time for rest and personal activities.

b. Distraction-Free Environment

Create a distraction-free work environment. Use tools like noise-canceling headphones, and inform family or housemates of your work hours to minimize interruptions.

Tools for Time Tracking and Project Management

Using the right tools can significantly enhance your time management and productivity. Here are some essential tools for time tracking and project management:

1. Time Tracking Tools

a. Toggl

Toggl is a simple and intuitive time tracking tool that helps you monitor how much time you spend on each task. It offers features like:

- **Timer:** Start and stop timers for different tasks.

- **Reports:** Generate detailed reports to analyze your time usage.
- **Integrations:** Integrate with other project management tools for seamless workflow.

b. Clockify

Clockify is a free time tracking tool that allows you to track time, manage projects, and generate reports. Key features include:

- **Timer and Manual Entry:** Track time in real-time or enter it manually.
- **Project Tracking:** Monitor time spent on different projects and tasks.
- **Reports:** Create visual reports to understand your time usage.

2. Project Management Tools

a. Trello

Trello is a visual project management tool that uses boards, lists, and cards to organize tasks. Features include:

- **Kanban Boards:** Visualize tasks in different stages of completion.
- **Collaboration:** Collaborate with team members by assigning tasks and adding comments.
- **Integrations:** Integrate with other tools like Slack, Google Drive, and more.

b. Asana

Asana is a comprehensive project management tool that helps you manage tasks, projects, and workflows. Features include:

- **Task Management:** Create tasks, assign them to team members, and set due dates.
- **Project Timelines:** Use timelines to visualize project progress and deadlines.
- **Collaboration:** Collaborate with team members through comments, attachments, and project updates.

c. Notion

Notion is an all-in-one workspace that combines note-taking, project management, and collaboration. Features include:

- **Customizable Pages:** Create pages for notes, tasks, databases, and more.
- **Templates:** Use templates for project management, personal productivity, and team collaboration.
- **Integrations:** Integrate with tools like Slack, Google Drive, and more.

Avoiding Burnout

Balancing multiple freelance gigs and projects can be demanding, and it's important to take steps to avoid burnout. Here are some strategies to help you maintain your well-being:

1. Take Regular Breaks

a. Pomodoro Technique

The Pomodoro Technique involves working for 25 minutes, followed by a 5-minute break.

After four cycles, take a longer break of 15-30 minutes. This helps maintain focus and prevent fatigue.

b. Stretch and Move

During breaks, take time to stretch, move around, and give your eyes a rest from screens. Physical activity can help refresh your mind and body.

2. Practice Self-Care

a. Healthy Habits

Maintain healthy habits such as regular exercise, a balanced diet, and adequate sleep. These habits contribute to overall well-being and productivity.

b. Mindfulness and Relaxation

Incorporate mindfulness practices like meditation, deep breathing exercises, or yoga into your routine. These practices can help reduce stress and improve focus.

3. Set Realistic Expectations

a. Manage Workload

Be realistic about how much work you can handle. Avoid overcommitting and learn to say no to additional projects if your workload is already full.

b. Quality Over Quantity

Focus on delivering high-quality work rather than taking on too many projects. Quality work can lead to repeat clients and referrals, reducing the need to constantly seek new gigs.

4. Seek Support

a. Professional Network

Build a network of fellow freelancers and remote workers who can offer support, advice, and collaboration opportunities. Sharing experiences and challenges can help reduce feelings of isolation.

b. Delegate When Possible

If you have the resources, consider delegating tasks to others. This can free up time for higher-priority work and help you manage your workload more effectively.

By planning and scheduling your workday, using time tracking and project management tools, and taking steps to avoid burnout, you can balance multiple freelance gigs and projects successfully. Effective time management and productivity strategies are essential for maintaining high performance and delivering quality work to all your clients. Remember to prioritize self-care and seek support when needed to sustain a long and fulfilling freelance career.

Chapter 11: Organizing Your Work

Effectively organizing your work is crucial for managing multiple clients and projects as a freelancer. By implementing efficient workflows, managing client expectations, and documenting processes and procedures, you can ensure smooth operations and high-quality deliverables. This chapter will guide you through essential strategies for organizing your work to achieve productivity and client satisfaction.

Managing Multiple Clients and Projects

Balancing multiple clients and projects requires a systematic approach to ensure that each task is completed on time and to a high standard.

1. Client Prioritization

a. Assess Project Scope and Deadlines

Evaluate the scope and deadlines of each project.

Prioritize tasks based on urgency, complexity, and the client's expectations.

b. Importance vs. Urgency

Use the Eisenhower Matrix to categorize tasks:

- **Urgent and Important:** Focus on these tasks first.
- **Important but Not Urgent:** Schedule these tasks for later.
- **Urgent but Not Important:** Delegate or minimize these tasks.
- **Not Urgent and Not Important:** Eliminate or defer these tasks.

c. Communication with Clients

Maintain clear and regular communication with your clients. Set expectations regarding response times, availability, and progress updates to avoid misunderstandings.

2. Task Management Systems

a. Task Lists

Create detailed task lists for each project. Break down larger tasks into smaller, manageable subtasks. Use digital tools like Todoist, Microsoft To Do, or simple spreadsheets.

b. Calendar Management

Use a calendar to schedule tasks and deadlines. Google Calendar, Outlook, or Apple Calendar can help you visualize your workload and avoid scheduling conflicts.

c. Weekly Reviews

Conduct weekly reviews to assess your progress and adjust your plans. This helps you stay on track and make necessary changes to your schedule.

Creating Efficient Workflows

Efficient workflows streamline your processes, saving time and reducing errors.

1. Workflow Mapping

a. Visualize Your Process

Map out your workflows visually using flowcharts or diagrams. Tools like Lucidchart, Miro, or even simple whiteboards can help you visualize each step.

b. Identify Bottlenecks

Analyze your workflows to identify bottlenecks and areas for improvement. Look for steps that cause delays or require excessive effort.

2. Automate Repetitive Tasks

a. Automation Tools

Use automation tools like Zapier, Integromat, or IFTTT to automate repetitive tasks. For example, automatically save email attachments to cloud storage or schedule social media posts.

b. Email Templates

Create email templates for common responses, project updates, or client inquiries. This saves time and ensures consistent communication.

3. Standardize Processes

a. Checklists

Develop checklists for recurring tasks and processes. Checklists help ensure that no steps are missed and maintain consistency across projects.

b. Templates

Create templates for proposals, invoices, project plans, and other documents. Templates save time and ensure a professional presentation.

Documenting Processes and Procedures

Documenting your processes and procedures provides clarity and consistency, especially as your workload grows.

1. Create Standard Operating Procedures (SOPs)

a. Detailed Instructions

Write detailed instructions for each process. Include step-by-step guidance, tools needed, and any relevant resources.

b. Visual Aids

Incorporate visual aids like screenshots, diagrams, or videos to enhance understanding. Tools like Snagit or Loom can help create visual documentation.

2. Organize Documentation

a. Centralized Repository

Store all documentation in a centralized, accessible location. Cloud storage solutions like Google Drive, Dropbox, or Notion are ideal for organizing and sharing documents.

b. Categorize and Tag

Categorize and tag your documents for easy retrieval. Use folders, labels, and tags to keep your documentation organized.

3. Regular Updates

a. Review and Revise

Regularly review and update your documentation to ensure it remains accurate and relevant. Schedule periodic reviews to incorporate any changes or improvements in your processes.

b. Feedback and Improvement

Encourage feedback from clients and team members on your processes. Use their insights to refine and enhance your workflows and documentation.

Tools for Organization and Efficiency

Using the right tools can significantly enhance your ability to organize and manage your work.

1. Project Management Tools

a. Trello

Trello uses boards, lists, and cards to help you organize tasks visually. It's ideal for managing multiple projects and collaborating with clients or team members.

b. Asana

Asana offers comprehensive project management features, including task assignments, deadlines, and project timelines. It's suitable for complex projects with multiple stakeholders.

c. Notion

Notion is an all-in-one workspace that combines note-taking, project management, and collaboration.

It's highly customizable, allowing you to create tailored workflows and documentation systems.

2. Communication Tools

a. Slack

Slack is a messaging platform that facilitates real-time communication and collaboration. Create channels for different projects or clients to keep conversations organized.

b. Microsoft Teams

Microsoft Teams integrates with Office 365, providing chat, video conferencing, and file-sharing capabilities. It's ideal for seamless collaboration within the Microsoft ecosystem.

3. Document Management Tools

a. Google Workspace

Google Workspace offers cloud-based tools for document creation, storage, and collaboration.

Use Google Docs, Sheets, and Drive to create and share project documents.

b. Dropbox

Dropbox provides secure cloud storage and file-sharing capabilities. Use it to organize and share large files or collaborate with clients and team members.

By managing multiple clients and projects efficiently, creating effective workflows, and documenting your processes and procedures, you can enhance your productivity and deliver high-quality work consistently. Utilizing the right tools and maintaining clear communication with clients are key to staying organized and meeting your professional goals as a freelancer.

Chapter 12: Financial Management for Freelancers

Managing finances effectively is critical for freelancers to maintain stability and growth in their careers. This chapter will cover essential aspects of financial management, including budgeting and saving, invoicing and getting paid on time, and understanding taxes and legal considerations.

Budgeting and Saving

Effective budgeting and saving strategies help freelancers manage irregular income and prepare for future financial needs.

1. Create a Budget

a. Track Income and Expenses

Start by tracking all your income sources and expenses.

Use tools like Mint, YNAB (You Need a Budget), or a simple spreadsheet to categorize and monitor your financial transactions.

b. Categorize Expenses

Divide your expenses into categories such as:

- **Fixed Expenses:** Rent, utilities, insurance, subscriptions.
- **Variable Expenses:** Groceries, transportation, entertainment.
- **Business Expenses:** Software, marketing, professional development.

c. Set Budget Limits

Set realistic limits for each expense category based on your income and financial goals. Review and adjust these limits regularly to reflect changes in your financial situation.

2. Build an Emergency Fund

a. Importance of an Emergency Fund

An emergency fund provides financial security during periods of low income or unexpected expenses. Aim to save at least three to six months' worth of living expenses.

b. How to Save

- **Automate Savings:** Set up automatic transfers to a separate savings account.
- **Cut Unnecessary Expenses:** Identify and eliminate non-essential expenses to boost your savings.

3. Plan for Taxes and Retirement

a. Estimate Tax Payments

Freelancers need to set aside a portion of their income for taxes. Estimate your tax liability and set aside money regularly to avoid a large tax bill at the end of the year.

b. Retirement Savings

Consider opening a retirement account such as an IRA (Individual Retirement Account) or a solo 401(k). Contribute regularly to build your retirement savings over time.

Invoicing and Getting Paid on Time

Timely and accurate invoicing is crucial for maintaining cash flow and ensuring you get paid for your work.

1. Create Professional Invoices

a. Essential Elements of an Invoice

Include the following elements in your invoices:

- **Your Business Information:** Name, address, email, phone number.
- **Client Information:** Name, address, email.
- **Invoice Number:** Unique identifier for each invoice.
- **Invoice Date:** Date the invoice is issued.
- **Due Date:** Payment due date.
- **Description of Services:**

Detailed description of the services provided.

- **Total Amount Due:** Clear breakdown of the charges and the total amount due.
- **Payment Terms:** Specify payment terms, including methods of payment and any late fees.

b. Invoicing Software

Use invoicing software like FreshBooks, QuickBooks, or Wave to create and send professional invoices. These tools also help you track payments and manage your finances.

2. Establish Clear Payment Terms

a. Upfront Payments and Milestones

Consider requesting upfront payments or setting milestones for larger projects. This ensures you receive partial payments throughout the project, reducing financial risk.

b. Late Fees and Penalties

Clearly state your policy on late payments, including any fees or penalties for overdue invoices. This encourages clients to pay on time.

3. Follow Up on Overdue Invoices

a. Send Reminders

Send polite reminders to clients for overdue invoices. Use invoicing software to automate reminders and follow-up emails.

b. Communication

Communicate with clients to understand any payment delays and negotiate a payment plan if necessary. Maintaining a professional and understanding approach can help resolve payment issues.

Taxes and Legal Considerations

Understanding taxes and legal obligations is essential for freelancers to stay compliant and avoid legal issues.

1. Understand Your Tax Obligations

a. Self-Employment Taxes

Freelancers are responsible for paying self-employment taxes, which cover Social Security and Medicare. Calculate your estimated tax payments and set aside money regularly.

b. Quarterly Estimated Taxes

Freelancers must pay quarterly estimated taxes to the IRS. Use Form 1040-ES to calculate and submit these payments.

c. State and Local Taxes

Be aware of state and local tax obligations, which vary depending on your location. Research the specific requirements for your area.

2. Keep Detailed Records

a. Income and Expense Tracking

Maintain detailed records of all income and expenses. Use accounting software or spreadsheets to organize your financial information.

b. Receipts and Documentation

Keep receipts and documentation for all business-related expenses. These records are essential for tax deductions and audits.

3. Business Structure and Legal Considerations

a. Choose a Business Structure

Decide on a business structure that suits your needs, such as a sole proprietorship, LLC (Limited Liability Company), or corporation. Each structure has different tax implications and legal protections.

b. Register Your Business

Register your business with the appropriate state and local authorities. Obtain any necessary licenses or permits to operate legally.

c. Contracts and Agreements

Use contracts and agreements to protect yourself and your business. Clearly outline the terms and conditions of your services, including payment terms, project scope, and deliverables.

d. Insurance

Consider obtaining business insurance, such as liability insurance, to protect against potential legal claims or disputes.

By implementing effective budgeting and saving strategies, creating professional invoices, and understanding your tax and legal obligations, you can manage your finances successfully as a freelancer. Proper financial management ensures stability and growth in your freelance career, allowing you to focus on delivering high-quality work to your clients.

Chapter 13: Maintaining Work-Life Balance

Achieving a healthy work-life balance is essential for freelancers to maintain their well-being and productivity. This chapter focuses on setting boundaries and expectations, finding time for personal growth and learning, and balancing work and personal life.

Setting Boundaries and Expectations

Setting clear boundaries and expectations is crucial for preventing work from encroaching on your personal life and ensuring that you have time to recharge.

1. Define Your Work Hours

a. Fixed Work Hours

Establish fixed work hours and stick to them.

This creates a clear separation between work time and personal time, helping you to focus during work hours and relax during personal time.

b. Flexible Schedule

If a fixed schedule isn't possible, set a daily or weekly work schedule that accommodates your personal commitments. Be consistent in your work hours to build a routine.

2. Communicate Boundaries

a. Inform Clients

Inform clients of your work hours and availability. Include this information in your email signature, contracts, and initial communications to set clear expectations.

b. Set Response Times

Set realistic response times for emails and messages.

Let clients know when they can expect to hear back from you to manage their expectations.

3. Create a Dedicated Workspace

a. Separate Work Area

Create a dedicated workspace that is separate from your living areas. This physical separation helps to mentally distinguish between work and personal time.

b. Ergonomic Setup

Invest in an ergonomic setup with a comfortable chair, desk, and proper lighting to improve your productivity and reduce physical strain.

4. Learn to Say No

a. Assess Workload

Regularly assess your workload to ensure you are not overcommitting.

Learn to say no to additional projects if they will compromise your work-life balance.

b. Prioritize Important Tasks

Focus on high-priority tasks and delegate or decline tasks that are not essential. This helps you maintain a manageable workload.

Finding Time for Personal Growth and Learning

Continuous learning and personal growth are important for staying competitive and fulfilled as a freelancer.

1. Schedule Learning Time

a. Allocate Regular Time Slots

Allocate specific time slots for learning and personal development. Treat this time as you would any other work commitment to ensure it is not overlooked.

b. Use Downtime Wisely

Use downtime or less busy periods to engage in learning activities. This helps you make the most of your time without compromising your work schedule.

2. Identify Learning Resources

a. Online Courses and Webinars

Enroll in online courses and webinars related to your field. Platforms like Coursera, Udemy, and LinkedIn Learning offer a wide range of courses.

b. Books and Articles

Read books and articles to stay updated on industry trends and best practices. Create a reading list and set aside time for reading regularly.

3. Network and Learn from Others

a. Join Professional Groups

Join professional groups and associations in your industry. Participate in discussions, attend events, and learn from the experiences of others.

b. Find a Mentor

Seek out a mentor who can provide guidance and support. A mentor can offer valuable insights and help you navigate challenges in your freelance career.

4. Practice Self-Reflection

a. Set Personal Goals

Set personal and professional development goals. Regularly review your progress and adjust your goals as needed.

b. Reflect on Experiences

Take time to reflect on your experiences and identify areas for improvement. Self-reflection helps you learn from your successes and challenges.

Balancing Work and Personal Life

Balancing work and personal life is essential for maintaining overall well-being and happiness.

1. Prioritize Self-Care

a. Physical Health

Maintain a healthy lifestyle by prioritizing physical health. Exercise regularly, eat a balanced diet, and get enough sleep.

b. Mental Health

Take care of your mental health by practicing mindfulness, meditation, or other relaxation techniques. Seek professional help if needed.

2. Make Time for Hobbies and Interests

a. Schedule Personal Time

Schedule time for hobbies and interests outside of work.

Engaging in activities you enjoy helps reduce stress and improve your overall well-being.

b. Explore New Activities

Try new activities and experiences to keep life interesting and fulfilling. This can also help you meet new people and expand your social network.

3. Spend Quality Time with Loved Ones

a. Plan Activities Together

Plan regular activities with family and friends. This helps strengthen your relationships and provides a break from work-related stress.

b. Unplug and Be Present

Unplug from work during personal time. Put away electronic devices and focus on being present with your loved ones.

4. Practice Work-Life Integration

a. Flexible Integration

Integrate work and personal life in a way that suits you. For example, you might work early in the morning and spend afternoons with your family.

b. Set Realistic Expectations

Set realistic expectations for what you can achieve in both work and personal life. Avoid trying to do everything at once and focus on what matters most.

By setting boundaries and expectations, finding time for personal growth and learning, and balancing work and personal life, you can maintain a healthy work-life balance as a freelancer. This balance is crucial for sustaining long-term success and happiness in your freelance career.

Chapter 14: Scaling Your Freelance Business

As you gain experience and build a steady client base, you might find it beneficial to scale your freelance business. Scaling can lead to increased revenue, more significant opportunities, and a more sustainable career. This chapter explores hiring subcontractors and virtual assistants, expanding your service offerings, long-term planning and goal setting, and concludes with final thoughts on your freelance journey.

Hiring Subcontractors and Virtual Assistants

Bringing on additional help can free up your time, allowing you to focus on high-value tasks and grow your business.

1. Identifying the Need

a. Assess Workload

Evaluate your current workload to determine if you need additional help. Look for tasks that are repetitive, time-consuming, or outside your core competencies.

b. Define Roles and Responsibilities

Clearly define the roles and responsibilities of subcontractors and virtual assistants. Determine which tasks can be delegated to free up your time.

2. Finding and Hiring

a. Sourcing Talent

Use platforms like Upwork, Fiverr, and LinkedIn to find qualified subcontractors and virtual assistants. Network within your industry for referrals.

b. Vetting Candidates

Conduct thorough interviews and review portfolios or past work to ensure candidates meet your standards.

Look for reliability, relevant experience, and strong communication skills.

c. Onboarding Process

Develop an onboarding process that includes training and clear instructions. Provide necessary tools and access to systems they will use.

3. Managing and Communicating

a. Set Expectations

Clearly communicate your expectations regarding deadlines, quality of work, and communication. Use contracts to formalize these expectations.

b. Regular Check-ins

Schedule regular check-ins to monitor progress, provide feedback, and address any issues. Use project management tools to track tasks and deadlines.

c. Foster a Collaborative Environment

Create an environment where subcontractors and virtual assistants feel valued and motivated. Encourage open communication and collaboration.

Expanding Your Service Offerings

Diversifying your services can attract new clients and increase your revenue streams.

1. Analyze Market Demand

a. Client Feedback

Listen to client feedback to identify potential areas for expanding your services. Understand their pain points and unmet needs.

b. Market Research

Conduct market research to identify trends and demands in your industry. Look for gaps in the market that you can fill with new services.

2. Develop New Skills

a. Continuous Learning

Invest in learning new skills that complement your current offerings. Take online courses, attend workshops, and stay updated with industry developments.

b. Certification and Training

Consider obtaining certifications or specialized training to enhance your credibility and attract new clients.

3. Introduce New Services

a. Pilot Programs

Start with pilot programs to test new services. Offer these to a select group of clients at a discounted rate in exchange for feedback.

b. Marketing New Services

Promote your new services through your website, social media, and email marketing.

Highlight the benefits and unique value of these services.

c. Bundle Services

Create service packages that bundle your existing and new offerings. This can provide more value to clients and increase your average transaction size.

Long-Term Planning and Goal Setting

Long-term planning and goal setting are essential for sustainable growth and success.

1. Set SMART Goals

a. Specific

Define clear and specific goals for your business. Avoid vague objectives and focus on precise outcomes.

b. Measurable

Ensure your goals are measurable.

Establish metrics and KPIs to track your progress.

c. Achievable

Set realistic and attainable goals based on your current resources and capabilities.

d. Relevant

Align your goals with your overall business vision and objectives. Ensure they are relevant to your long-term success.

e. Time-bound

Set deadlines for achieving your goals. This creates a sense of urgency and helps you stay focused.

2. Create a Business Plan

a. Vision and Mission

Articulate your vision and mission statements. These guide your business decisions and strategies.

b. Market Analysis

Conduct a thorough market analysis to understand your target audience, competitors, and market conditions.

c. Financial Projections

Develop financial projections to forecast your revenue, expenses, and profitability. This helps you plan for growth and allocate resources effectively.

d. Marketing Strategy

Outline your marketing strategy to attract and retain clients. Include online and offline marketing tactics.

3. Review and Adjust

a. Regular Reviews

Conduct regular reviews of your goals and business plan. Assess your progress and identify areas for improvement.

b. Adjust Strategies

Be flexible and adjust your strategies based on changing market conditions, client feedback, and business performance.

c. Celebrate Achievements

Celebrate your achievements and milestones. Recognize the progress you've made and use it as motivation to continue growing.

Conclusion

Scaling your freelance business requires careful planning, strategic decision-making, and effective management. By hiring subcontractors and virtual assistants, expanding your service offerings, and setting long-term goals, you can achieve sustainable growth and greater success in your freelance career.

Final Thoughts

Embrace the challenges and opportunities that come with freelancing. Remember that continuous learning, adaptability, and a focus on delivering value to your clients are key to your long-term success. As you scale your business, maintain the work-life balance that allows you to thrive both personally and professionally. Your freelance journey is unique, and with dedication and strategic planning, you can build a successful and fulfilling career.

Chapter 15: Conclusion

As we wrap up this guide on building and scaling a successful freelance career, it's essential to reflect on your journey, anticipate future trends in freelancing and remote work, and explore resources for continued learning and growth. This chapter will help you consolidate your experiences, prepare for future opportunities, and stay updated in an ever-evolving industry.

Reflecting on Your Freelance Journey

1. Assessing Your Progress

a. Review Your Achievements

Take time to reflect on your accomplishments since starting your freelance career. Consider the projects you've completed, the skills you've developed, and the relationships you've built with clients.

b. Identify Challenges and Lessons Learned

Acknowledge the challenges you've faced and the lessons you've learned from them. Understanding these experiences will help you grow and improve as a freelancer.

c. Evaluate Your Growth

Assess your professional and personal growth. Have you achieved the goals you set for yourself? How have your priorities and aspirations evolved?

2. Celebrate Milestones

a. Recognize Milestones

Celebrate significant milestones in your freelance journey, such as landing your first client, reaching a revenue goal, or expanding your services. Recognizing these achievements can boost your motivation and confidence.

b. Share Success with Others

Share your successes with your network, including clients, colleagues, friends, and family.

Their support and encouragement can be invaluable as you continue to grow.

3. Plan for the Future

a. Set New Goals

Based on your reflections, set new goals for your freelance business. Consider both short-term objectives and long-term aspirations.

b. Adapt and Innovate

Stay adaptable and open to new ideas and opportunities. The freelance landscape is constantly changing, and innovation is key to staying relevant and successful.

Future Trends in Freelancing and Remote Work

1. Increasing Demand for Freelancers

a. Rise of the Gig Economy

The gig economy is expanding, with more businesses turning to freelancers for specialized skills and flexible work arrangements. This trend is expected to continue, providing ample opportunities for freelancers.

b. Remote Work Normalization

The normalization of remote work, accelerated by the COVID-19 pandemic, has led to greater acceptance and integration of remote freelancers into various industries. This shift offers more flexibility and access to global markets.

2. Technological Advancements

a. AI and Automation

Advancements in AI and automation are transforming various aspects of freelancing, from project management to client communication. Staying updated with these technologies can enhance your efficiency and competitiveness.

b. Online Collaboration Tools

Improved online collaboration tools are making it easier for freelancers to work with clients and teams across the globe. Familiarize yourself with the latest tools and platforms to streamline your workflow.

3. Evolving Client Expectations

a. Value-Driven Services

Clients are increasingly looking for freelancers who provide value-driven services, focusing on outcomes and results rather than just completing tasks. Demonstrating your impact on clients' businesses will be crucial.

b. Personalized Client Experiences

Providing personalized and exceptional client experiences can set you apart from competitors. Building strong relationships and understanding clients' unique needs will become even more important.

4. Emphasis on Work-Life Balance

a. Flexible Work Arrangements

The demand for flexible work arrangements is growing, with both freelancers and clients prioritizing work-life balance. Embrace this trend by maintaining a healthy balance and setting boundaries.

b. Mental Health Awareness

Greater awareness of mental health and well-being is influencing how freelancers manage their careers. Prioritize self-care and mental health to sustain long-term success.

Resources for Continued Learning and Growth

1. Online Learning Platforms

a. Coursera, Udemy, and LinkedIn Learning

These platforms offer a wide range of courses on various topics, from technical skills to business management.

Continuously investing in your education will help you stay competitive.

b. Skillshare

Skillshare provides creative and practical courses taught by industry experts. Explore classes that align with your interests and professional goals.

2. Industry Conferences and Webinars

a. Virtual Conferences

Participate in virtual industry conferences and webinars to stay updated on trends, network with peers, and gain insights from industry leaders.

b. Specialized Events

Attend specialized events related to your niche or industry. These events offer valuable opportunities for learning and networking.

3. Professional Associations and Communities

a. Freelancers Union

Join professional associations like the Freelancers Union for resources, advocacy, and networking opportunities. Engage with the community to share experiences and learn from others.

b. Online Communities and Forums

Participate in online communities and forums related to freelancing and your specific industry. Platforms like Reddit, Quora, and specialized forums offer valuable advice and support.

4. Books and Publications

a. Recommended Reading

Stay informed by reading books and publications on freelancing, business, and personal development. Some recommended titles include "The Freelancer's Bible" by Sara Horowitz and "The 4-Hour Workweek" by Tim Ferriss.

b. Industry Journals and Blogs

Follow industry journals and blogs to keep up with the latest trends and best practices. Subscribing to newsletters and RSS feeds can help you stay updated.

Conclusion

Your freelance journey is a unique and rewarding experience that offers endless opportunities for growth and success. By reflecting on your progress, anticipating future trends, and leveraging resources for continued learning, you can build a thriving freelance career that aligns with your personal and professional goals.

Final Thoughts

Freelancing is not just a career choice; it's a lifestyle that offers flexibility, independence, and the potential for significant personal and professional growth. Embrace the challenges and opportunities that come your way, stay committed to delivering value to your clients, and continue investing in your development.

With dedication and strategic planning, you can achieve lasting success and fulfillment in your freelance career.

www.ingramcontent.com/pod-product-compliance
Lightning Source LLC
Chambersburg PA
CBHW071922210526
45479CB00002B/518